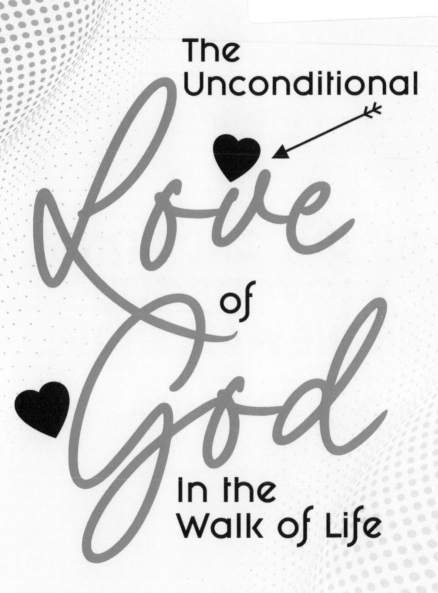

The Unconditional Love of God In the Walk of Life

Naledi Phaladi

Design & Drawings; Mompati Serojane and Ray Fliq

THE UNCONDITIONAL LOVE OF GOD IN THE WALK OF LIFE

NALEDI PHALADI

Scriptures and quotes are from:
The NIV Soul Survivor Youth Bible
The Holy Bible, new international version®NIV®
Copyright © 1979, 1984, 2011 by biblica Inc.
Used by permission. All rights reserved worldwide.

Design & Drawings: Mompati Serojane and Ray Fliq

ISBN:

CONTENTS
Dedication i

DEDICATION

This book is dedicated to everyone especially the youth and the young generation who want to learn, grow, their unconditional love of God in their walk of life.

May the Lord grant you all, Amen.

ACKNOWLEDGEMENT.

Above all things, I would like to thank God. Lord, thank you for this opportunity that I am able to share the unconditional love of God with others. Help them understand, grow, and be nurtured in your love in their walks of life.

Secondly, I would like to thank my family for the encouragement they have given me, that I have now accomplished what God has asked me to do.

To my editor, Christian Book Editor Ltd (Amos Adekayero), thank you so much. I appreciate your efforts.

To my book designers and illustrators: Mompati Serojane and Ray Fliq, I would like to express my gratitude and say thank you so much. I am forever grateful. Words cannot explain how much thankful I am.
Ke a leboga.

Chapter One

RELATIONSHIP WITH GOD

The relationship with God is not only on Christmas Day nor Easter, or on a Sunday at church listening to the word of God, which most forget about during the week. We as Christians need to develop this daily—every hour and minute during our walk of life. Let us nurture this relationship like the growth of a tree by watering, pruning, and taking care of it in the walk of Jesus. An example from the Bible is Mathew 4 v 4 and Luke 4 v 4. They support this by stating that "man cannot leave by bread alone but on every word that comes from God''. This statement clearly states that we as individuals should live by the word of God every single day and put God first in what we do.

In times of hardship, people should have a relationship with Jesus as He is one of the best people who will love you for who you are and will never judge you. He is the one with a reliable shoulder to cry on; He loves the broken-hearted. He will mend and put you as a whole (holistic approach). An example from Psalm 147 v 3 is, "He heals the broken-hearted and binds up their wounds". So, put Him at the centre of your lives (person-centred).

Having a relationship with Jesus will make a person live in peace despite what may be happening in the world. God's love is genuine. He also emphasises that we should love others as we love ourselves and as God has loved us. He showed us this by sending His only begotten Son (Jesus) to the world for us so that we can have eternal life (John 3:16).

Love of God
Jesus, the Son of God, loved us unconditionally, and this understanding of His love can be compared to the tree of life. An example from the gospel of John chapter 15 v 5 says He is the vine, and we are the branches. It says if we remain in Him and Him in us

our lives will be fruitful, and we will live with joy because of the love of God. However, if people decide not to remain in Him, they will have nothing. They will live in fear, lacking understanding, and will not be aware of His love. Remaining in Him leads to His glory and walking in faith. Therefore, the love of God can be shown by following the Ten Commandments, walking in obedience, loving one another, and becoming His friend. Also, becoming His best friend is attainable. In John Chapter 15 verse 14, it states that we are His friends if we do what He commands.

Summary

God's love is rooted in a foundation that needs to be taken care of throughout the walk of life. For example, it needs to be built on solid ground for it to grow. The growth of faith and His love endures forever in our lives. The Lord will protect us from the plagues and diseases. Knowing that there is someone to trust even if we don't understand is a succour to our souls. God's timing is always the best. Whilst a person is living their lives, they should remember the God of Abraham, merge their lifestyle with the Lord, and walk with Him in every situation.

Chapter Two

GETTING TO KNOW GOD AND TRUSTING HIM

God knew us before we were formed and had a plan for each one of us. First, He prepared the way by creating the heavens and the earth, ensuring that everything is there in the pathway from the beginning. From this, God made creations like the moon, flowers, and stars.

God is the bread of life, and those who come to Him shall not be hungry or thirsty but have eternal life. John chapter 6 verse 35 says:

"I am the bread of life, whoever comes to me will never go hungry and thirsty".

Getting to know God is being obedient to Him and staying with people who know Him; as such company can nurture and tell you about His love and presence. They will also encourage you to be nurtured in His love. He will show you the way and make you positive, faithful,and fruitful. As an individual, you have to meditate on His words, show understanding, and ask Him to help you when you do not understand. Ask, and it shall be given to you, knock and the door shall open (Mathew 7.7), and seek ye the kingdom of God. Worship His songs in His presence, start your day with a refreshing positive attitude, and make it a habit to call to Him first thing in the morning when you wake up. Avoid going to your phone first. Don't make it a habit; let us build a nation of Christ. Therefore, know God first and pour your heart unto Him. Make Him understand. Trust that His love endures forever.

At times, it is being involved where His love is, assisting others, or just the small little things that will help you as well. For example, in John chapter 1 v 1, it says, "In the beginning was the Word, and the Word was with God, and the Word was God". Psalm 46 v 10, on the other hand, asks us to be still and know that there is God. Therefore, it is our responsibility as individuals to strive to know Him and trust His process.

Trusting God
Trusting God is laying all your understanding on Him even though you don't understand.

Psalms 37 v 3 (NIV) goes like this: "Trust in the Lord and do good; dwell in the land and enjoy safe pasture. Take delight in the Lord and he will give you the desires of heart."

As seen in the verse, we need to put all our trust in Him because He will keep us safe and give you what you ask Him. On the other hand, in whatever you do, make sure you put God first and trust Him to shine His light in the darkness of your life. For example, amid this pandemic (Covid-19), all you need to do is put all your trust in Him. He will make a way when the time is right. There will be healing, and whilst trusting Him, have faith, and all shall be well. Be at peace and keep trusting Him. The Book of Jeremiah 17 verse 7 says blessed are the ones who trust and have confidence in the Lord. When plagues come in, they will stay firm and not be shaken by anything because their trust and faith in the Lord have bonded them together.

John 14 v 6 says Christ is the way, the truth, and the life, and no one comes to His Father except through Him. The Book of 1 Corinthians 8 v 3 tells us that whoever loves God is known by Him. His love remains at the centre of our lives; therefore, we should know Him by trusting His process, walking in obedience, and spending time with Him every day, hour, and minute.

Therefore, Proverbs 3:5-6 concludes by saying:
"Trust in the Lord with all your heart and lean not on your own under-standing; in all your ways submit to him, and he will make your paths straight".

Summary
After knowing God, a person will live a happy, positive lifestyle because they know that God is there, and they are putting in all their Unconditional love of God in the walk of Life trust by obeying Him.

Chapter Three

THANKFUL AND GRATEFUL

In whatever you do, thank God. Be thankful and grateful each day.

From life experience

Dear God, I would like to say thank you for my life and for taking care of me. I am thankful for you. You are my everything; you are my stronghold. I am grateful and loved by your love. I am blessed, and I thank you for welcoming me. You are my strength, and I am proud to call you my best friend, God.

What are you thankful for?

....
....
....
....
....
....
....
....
....
....
....
....
....
....
....
....
....
....
....

Psalms 107 v 1 tells us that, "Give thanks to the Lord, for he is good; his love endures forever".

This verse shows us that we should give thanks, and He is good and forever grateful, as His love is ever-present—forever and ever. Thanks be to God. As individuals, we should give thanks to Him daily, in every place, being grateful for His love and thankful all the time.

What are you grateful for?

....
....
....
....
....
....
....
....
....
....
....
....
....
....
....
....
....
....
....
....
....
....
....
....
....
....
....
....
....

Chapter Four

FAITH

To walk with God, you must have faith. You cannot live a fearful and worried life all time. You have to trust the Lord with all your heart.When plagues come upon the earth like in the year 2020, know that God is still with you. Thank Him all the time, and trust the process. As a young person, you have to leave the distraction behind and walk in faith with the Lord. The year 2020 has shown that His words are indeed love. We see quarantine in Isaiah 26:20: "Go, home my people enter your rooms and shut the doors behind you; hide yourselves for a little while until his wrath has passed by.''

This verse links with the beginning of 2020, and throughout the months of 2020, people saw what was unusual on the earth—the world was quarantined. Lockdown was introduced throughout the nations of the earth due to a pandemic (Covid-19) that emerged and changed how people live. This pandemic brought fear, confusion, and panic in people as it shut every service apart from the essential services. But by faith, God was with us by focusing on the positives and not living a fearful life.

In addition, Exodus 30:17-21 mentions the washing of hands, which clearly is being used for fighting this pandemic. Therefore, the Book of Exodus illustrates that those who had faith and obeyed the Lord were saved from the ten plagues sent to Egypt at the time of Moses.

In the beginning, God has formed the earth, and He did this in seven days and then rested (Genesis 2 v 2). Following this, Noah walked in faith with the Lord, and he was obedient to the Lord by listening to Him. However, when Noah informed people of a deluge coming over the earth, they did not listen to him. Instead, they laughed about it. Then the waters came and washed away every single thing that was not in the ark of Noah. Similarly, regarding the Covid-19 pandemic, people refused to listen—they were not wearing masks nor observing social distancing, as they believe this pandemic is not there.

Abraham was a man of faith who trusted the Lord and obeyed Him. Truthfully, he was faithful and obeyed the Lord and lived on God's word. Therefore, those who live in faith are not fearful of the pandemic as they walk with the Lord everywhere. When we walk with the Lord,we have to trust and obey. To add, Joshua 1:9 says, "...Be strong and courageous. Do not be afraid; do not be discouraged, for the LORD your God will be with you wherever you go."

Matthew 6:25-28 states that people should not worry about what they would eat or drink. They should be aware that God is the first point of contact. In other words, they should put God first in everything they do. For instance, Matthew 6:33 emphasises this by stating that,"But seek first his kingdom and his righteousness, and all these things will be given to you as well'', and "therefore do not worry about tomorrow, for tomorrow will worry about itself''. As a result, people should not worry about Covid-19, but in everything they do, they should first seek the kingdom of God, listen, trust, and obey Him.

In addition, we see in the Book of Deuteronomy, where God made the Israelites walk in the desert for 40 years with Moses because they continually refused to listen to the Lord and obey Him. And when the people did not obey the Lord, there were plagues in the world. An example is when Pharaoh refused to let the Israelites go. God punished Him (Pharaoh) with ten different plagues until he let them go on the last plague. The moral lesson is people should turn away from disobedience and love one another as God has loved each one of us. He emphasised this by stating on Deuteronomy 6 v 4, "Listen, O Israel! The Lord is our God, the Lord alone''. And '' you must love the Lord your God with all your heart...'' This can be compared to the year 2020, where we had different plagues throughout the month because people failed to obey the use of face masks, sanitisers, washing of hands, and social distancing.

Noah, on the other hand, was a man of faith. He walked in faith and obeyed the Lord by building an ark to save the remnants of the world when it flooded for 40 days and 40 nights. People refused to listen to Noah and did not enter the ark because they didn't believe his warnings and prophecy. It was a usual day for them. For example, Matthew 24:38-39 linked with this by stating that "For as in those days before the flood, they were eating and drinking...and they did not understand until the flood came and took them all away..." Just like the year 2020, people were not aware that Covid-19 could spread across the globe and bring new living conditions. At present, people still fail to understand that Covid-19 is still there, as they are still disobedient, just like in the time of Noah and Moses. In comparison to this, Abraham lived joyfully and obeyed the Lord, so did Noah.

In contrast, the lack of faith or small faith will make people doubt, just like Peter in Matthew 14 v 28-31. When Peter saw Jesus walk on water, it inspired him to say he wanted to do the same [to walk on water]. Later, he began to drown because of his little faith and fear, as he couldn't handle the wind and fierceness of the sea. So, he cried to Jesus to save him. In today's world, like the year 2020, if people are afraid of the virus, the Lord is calling you because He has seen your cries and wants you to walk with Him. He doesn't want you to be of little faith but to be faithful to Him always. Matthew 21 v 21 highlights that: "Truly I tell you, if you have faith and do not doubt, not only can you do what was done to the fig tree, but also you can say to this mountain, 'Go, throw yourself into the sea,' and it will be done."

Another example is from Matthew 8 v 23. Jesus was in a boat with His disciples, and somehow, He fell asleep, and a storm came. Water poured into the boat; the disciples became afraid, and they started to wake Jesus. Their faith was little. Jesus woke up and asked them where their faith was? He stopped the storm. Similarly, compared to the days of Covid-19, people need faith to be able to conquer this virus. Also, they need to trust God all the time.

When we have an illness, we need to walk in faith and believe that we will be healed. An example of this is from my personal life experience. I had suffered mental health, and I had no idea what was happening. It was a roller-coaster, but God healed me through my faith. God is able, hey you; yes, you have faith in God, and He will deliver. Ask, knock, and the door will be opened. Seek, and you shall find. I would encourage those suffering from mental health or any other diseases to have faith in the Lord. Be obedient, and you will be healed. Jeremiah

30 v 17 confirms that God can restore a person's health and heal their wounds. But Isaiah 38:16-17 says, "You restored me to health and let me live..." On the other hand, Jeremiah 33:6, mentions that "I will bring health and healing to it, I will heal my people and will let them enjoy abundant peace and security".

Chapter Five

PERSEVERANCE

What is perseverance?

Perseverance is when we take one step at a time with God. Unfortunately, most people often struggle with this. So, I encourage you to find other ways to persevere, no matter how hard it is. Try your best. Ask God to help you to persevere with Him every day. For it is written, knock, ask, and seek ye the kingdom of God.

The Book of Psalm 86 v 11 says, "Teach me your way, Lord, that I may rely on your faithfulness; give me an undivided heart, that I may fear your name." In this way, people will fear nothing, but their faith will save them from living in fear.

Another example is the Book of Lamentations 3:22-24, which teaches us that we are made new and not consumed because of God's love, and His compassion never fails. Therefore, people should be encouraged to live by God's love every new dawn or day and wait for God to renew their strength.

Perseverance is significant because we put our hope in the Lord and our faith in Him. Also, we wait for Him, just like it says in the Book of Lamentations.

Ways of overcoming perseverance
This can be done by asking God to teach us to walk by faith, not sight. 2 Corinthians 5 v 7 supports this statement. This life is about faith, not sight.

Nothing is impossible with God, but the word itself says I am possible. So, anything is possible, even perseverance. Therefore, stay faithful in the Lord.

In the end, you will rejoice in the Lord and be happy that you have overcome obstacles that were trying to stop you, circumstances making things difficult. Because you remained in faith, God has heard your cry.Be strong and courageous. Do not be afraid, for your Lord is with you wherever you go. Even in the midst of a storm, persevere and remain in His love, as it endures forever.

Summary
In life, we have to persevere, develop and make improvements to our way of life. In God, His love endures forever. Even if there are difficulties, with Christ, you will make it through. Just like Moses walking through the wilderness with the Israelites for 40 days and 40 nights, they reached the Promised Land with the help of God through Joshua. Now that we know God's love endures forever, we have the confidence that despite life difficulties, we will make it through Him.

Chapter Six

PATIENCE

Patience

Patience is a fruit of the Spirit that Christians should have. It can be applied every day in our daily lives.

Patience is when we wait without complaining. 1 Corinthians 13 tells us that love is patient, and patience is a vital ingredient of faith, hope, and love. They work together, and God's love is always expressed through patience.

Romans 12 v 12, on the other hand, says that being hopeful gives an individual joy, and people should be patient despite any plagues or difficulties they may encounter. We should be helpful to others, including the helpless.

As individuals, we need to wait for the Lord with patience. We should not be timid or proud to ask for help. When we do, it shall be given to us. Let's trust His process, for His love endures forever.

James 5 v 7 tells us that in the midst of suffering, we all should wait until the Lord comes. Let's take a look:

"Be patient, then, brothers and sisters, until the Lord's coming. See how the farmer waits for the land to yield its valuable crop, patiently waiting for the autumn and spring rains. You too, be patient and stand firm, because the Lord's coming is near."

Reflection
What have you learned from this chapter?

....
....
....
....
....
....
....
....
....
....
....
....
....
....
....
....
....
....
....

Do you think it will help you in moving forward with God?
Yes ...... No.....

Chapter Seven

WORSHIP

Worship can be in different forms. For example, Christians can worship God through singing, while some can worship Him through arts via drawings, colouring, journaling, and preaching. To be in worship, you need the presence of the Lord with the Spirit of the Lord. You must be in truth, become humble, and pay obeisance to His words throughout your life.

Singing

Isaiah 12 v 5-6:
"Sing to the LORD for he has done glorious things, let this be known to the world. Shout aloud and sing for joy, people of Zion, for great is the Holy One of Israel among you."

In comparison to today's world, people tend to block one of the ways of worshipping God through their inability to sing. I have witnessed a majority that says they can't sing, but with me being passionate about the unconditional love of God, I always advise that they should remove the "t" and say they can sing. Be positive about it and remove the negative things. For it is written in the Book of Isaiah to sing to the Lord.

Worship involves having God's unconditional love. Subdue that mind that is convincing you to think you can't sing. Be positive and say you can sing. Worship God like no other. Know that no one will judge you. Sing like no other; sing your heart out! Even if it's just nothing, it means the world. God will appreciate and allow you to be grateful under His wings, and you will soar like eagles and fly.

Journaling

Journaling can be another way of worshipping God; it will be just you and God. When you write to the Almighty in peace in your walk of life, write what's on your mind and talk to God. If you can't speak, write to Him; He will surely understand you.
Habakkuk 2: 2:
"...Write down the revelation and make it plain on tablets..."

The lord will surely instruct an individual what to do, whether is writing or journaling he will be in control of your life, so allow him to help you to walk with him through various routes.

Colouring/Drawings

A person can worship God through colours. God speaks to us in different ways, and colouring is one of those ways. He can also talk to us in drawings. You can show your unconditional love for Him through drawings, and He will understand the message being conveyed.

Preaching

An individual/preacher can preach to people by motivating them concerning the message preached on that particular day. Preachers can worship with individuals, and in this way, people get to worship God in church.

I hope my words of advice will help you worship God in your walk of life. Thank you.

Prayer

Dear God,
Thank you for loving me unconditionally;
I pray you show others ways in which your love is better than life
Guide them, oh Lord,
Let the grace of God lead them,
Let the light shine in the darkness,
Let the people be nurtured in your love,
Help them, oh Lord; help them to persevere,
Help them to understand your love,
Help them to have patience in you, oh God!
Let them know you and help them to grow and be able to stand
up for you, oh God!
Help them to overcome obstacles;
Open new doors, oh Lord, and make straight paths;
Help them to be independent by knowing you and having a
relationship with you;
Help them to worship you, oh Lord!
Help them to know how to give thanks to you,
As a way of saying thank you;
Help them, dear God,
To show appreciation to you, oh Lord!
Let them be in your presence, in Jesus' name;
Help them to walk in faith and believe that anything is possible
with God;
Let the grace of the Lord Jesus Christ and the love of God and
the fellowship of the Holy Spirit be with them evermore!

Amen ⊠

Poem

Unconditional love of God
Unconditional love
The unshakeable and pleasant love
An ever-present love with nothing hindering or stopping it
The love that requires listening and being obedient
The love that can take you places
The love that is untouchable
The love that requires an individual to obey
The love that is unstoppable
That is the kind of love God has.

He wants each and everyone to know His love. Through this book, you will learn, grow, and be nurtured under His love. You will know what you need to do to cherish His love and learn. In addition, you will also master how to live your life by God throughout your walk of life.

All thanks to God,
By Naledi

AUTHOR BIOGRAPHY

Naledi Phaladi is an author of : The Unconditional Love of God In the Walk of Life. She was born and raised in Botswana and stays in the UK. She loves God unconditionally. She loves singing,going for walks, writing: poetry,journaling and being creative.

THE END

The Unconditional Love of God In the Walk of Life

Do you want to experience the unconditional love of God in your life?

Have you ever experienced the unconditional love of God in your life?

This book targets the youth so they can cherish the unconditional love of God and put Him at the centre of their lives, looking unto the Lord. Reading this book will make you develop and understand His unconditional love in your walk of life. As a youth, you will be able to view God holistically, gain understanding, and be empathetic with Him in your life, knowing He is with you. It helps you with the step-by-step guide to take when loving God unconditionally throughout your life.

The Unconditional Love of God In The Walk of Life raises awareness of God's unconditional love in day-to-day living. It also has steps an individual (youth) can use to follow God and experience His unconditional love. This book is designed to change youth's lives so they can develop their unconditional love for God at a young age. Consequently, this will cause them to build a foundation and be wise in God's word on their earthly journey. It will unlock their potential by allowing them to reflect on it.

This book will assist the youth with:
Relationship with God
Getting to know God and Trusting Him
Thankful and Grateful
Faith
Perseverance
Patience
Worship

Printed in Great Britain
by Amazon

20824533R00018